Allegory of the Supermarket

POEMS BY

Stephanie Brown

The University of Georgia Press

ATHENS AND LONDON

Published by the University of Georgia Press
Athens, Georgia 30602
© 1998 by Stephanie Brown
All rights reserved

Designed by Betty Palmer McDaniel
Set in 11/13 Monotype Garamond
Printed and bound by McNaughton & Gunn

The paper in this book meets the guidelines
for permanence and durability of the Committee
on Production Guidelines for Book Longevity
of the Council on Library Resources.

Printed in the United States of America
02 01 00 99 98   P   5 4 3 2 1

Library of Congress Cataloging in Publication Data

Brown, Stephanie, 1961–
Allegory of the supermarket : poems / by Stephanie Brown.
p.   cm. — (Contemporary poetry series)
ISBN 0-8203-2068-4 (pbk. : alk. paper)
I. Title. II. Series: Contemporary poetry series
(University of Georgia Press)
PS3552.R723A79   1998
811'.54—dc21   98-25555
CIP

British Library Cataloging in Publication Data available

Allegory
of the Supermarket

To Derek Christiansen

As one still panting, ashore from dangerous seas,

Looks back at the deep he has escaped. . . .
—Dante, *Inferno,* Canto I,
trans. Robert Pinsky

"The amount of thought they give to their clothing,
the people who are afraid of looking frivolous!"

—Henry James, *The Bostonians*

ACKNOWLEDGMENTS

Grateful acknowledgment is made to the editors of the
following publications:

American Poetry Review
    "Parts of the Eye," "Interview with an Alchemist in the New
    Age," "Chapter One," "No Longer a Girl," "Reading True
    Crime Stories," "Kitsch," "Marginalia," "Fitness: A Triptych,"
    "No, No, Nostalgia!" "Schadenfreude," "Feminine Intuition,"
    "Allegory of the Supermarket," "The Zeitgeist," "The Role of
    the Female Artist in Society," "Fashion and the Fat Girl,"
    "Marriage," "I Was a Phony Baloney!" "Keeping Up with the
    Joneses," "The Lost Coast, California," "The Neighborhood
    of Successful Marriage," "Shamans," "Arrangement in Dark
    and Light," "A Gargoyle," "Mommy Is a Scary Narcissist"

Delmar
    "She Lay on the Bed in Tears"

Jacaranda Review
    "The Slow Hours"
Pavement
    "Aesthetic Questions"

Yellow Silk: Journal of the Erotic Arts
    "Boys," "Commencement Address," "Unfasten, Lift Up"

"Chapter One" was included in *The Best American Poetry 1993,*
edited by Louise Glück, series editor, David Lehman (Scribner).
"Schadenfreude" was included in *The Best American Poetry 1995,*
edited by Richard Howard, series editor, David Lehman
(Scribner). "Feminine Intuition" was included in *The Best
American Poetry 1997,* edited by James Tate, series editor, David
Lehman (Scribner).

CONTENTS

PART I: Feminine Intuition

Chapter One 3
Feminine Intuition 5
Schadenfreude 7
The Role of the Female Artist in Society 9
Fitness: A Triptych 10
I Was a Phony Baloney! 12
Marriage 13
Allegory of the Supermarket 14

PART II: Cataract Surgery

Parts of the Eye 19
The Slow Hours 22
Boys 23
The Kid from the Commune 25
Cataract Surgery 28
The Lost Coast, California 30
No, No, Nostalgia! 32

PART III: Marginalia

Reading True Crime Stories 37
Marginalia 38
Kitsch 40
Aesthetic Questions 42
It Took a Village 43
The Neighborhood of Successful Marriage 44
Fashion and the Fat Girl 45
Poetry 47
Interview with an Alchemist in the New Age 48

PART IV: No Longer a Girl

No Longer a Girl 53
Unfasten, Lift Up 55
She Lay on the Bed in Tears 56
Shamans 58
The Fourth of July 60
Five Sketches, in a Restaurant 62
Arrangement in Dark and Light 65
California 67
The Zeitgeist 69

PART V: Gargoyles

Keeping Up with the Joneses 73
A Gargoyle 75
Warm, Fuzzy 77
Mommy Is a Scary Narcissist 79
Schmooze . . . 81
Color Photo 83
Agapé 85
Commencement Address 87

Notes 89

I

Feminine Intuition

CHAPTER ONE

We librarians went to Baja last weekend and sat in the sun
Ho! Ho! It's funny, isn't it? Though not really Henry Jamesian
It's not so simple that we're prim and went to the exotic
Though perhaps that's what the story really is.
We librarians went to Baja last weekend and sat in the sun
and walked on the beach and played tennis at the Head
    Clerk's club
Though we were vacationing without hierarchy.
In this way I love my job, bureaucrat that I am, I love
to rank, to answer, to box; I love the Boolean in logic.
So perhaps that's why we went: Baja Mexico, if you've
    never been,
is about rusted cars growing into grass
on the side of the highway and shacks,
and roadside stands for olives and honey,
and Americans driving fast to the beach-and-tennis clubs
    they've built,
and the surfers in the ocean, waiting, rocking;
You see men standing in the no-man's land of the border,
waiting to cross: The border patrol jeeps with their rifles
ride by in the dust
Dirt roads and beer advertising everywhere
you look when you drive through Ensenada. We librarians
went to Baja last weekend and sat in the sun and we got a joke
    running:
what's the next fad in publishing after Co-Dependency?
It was a category of men who don't want to be success objects,
    we decided.
Self-help books for men who are eaten alive by women-mad-
    for-money.
You make them take a quiz, and everyone fits the category.

But my ex-boss, sitting there, and I are both in love with
     alcoholics,
She's married to hers and I've decided not to marry mine.
So maybe since we're prim and bookish we need the wild type—
I've thought about it. We laugh about these books
but just, just maybe. My ex-boss, now an administrator,
is the daughter of blacklisted Hollywood screenwriters.
She said they used to vacation right where we were when she was
     a kid.
They would dig for clams
in the bay that's going to be dredged into a marina for
     Americans.
Her family lived in exile, in Mexico.
She told me one day her husband doesn't believe those things
Really happened in America.
It's hard, though, to vacation without hierarchy.
Someone is the best tennis player, the best storyteller, the best
gossip, has the best body, gets along best. And you remember
where you stand as an employee. You remember
you're an American in a foreign country.
We librarians went to Baja and sat in the sun:
A day in the life, a *fête gallante*—
There was a house I wanted to run away from. Could I?

FEMININE INTUITION

I. Little Red Riding Hood

Astrid comes from upstate New York.
She comes from distress.
She's enthusiastic about it.
She doesn't belong, but she tries hard.
Her husband hurts her, but they have a drug-free life.
They roller skate and take up fads enthusiastically,
Neon clothing and the like.
He's an air traffic controller, so they move constantly.
This time it's California. After the picnic
I said, "She reminds me of Little Red Riding Hood."
My husband said, "Yeah."
We were doing the dishes.
I can't say some other things, so I say this.

II. Plastic Surgery, Skipped Dessert

That simple woman thought I was simple, but I was not.
I was never simple.
Not trees, stars, plot.
She smoked her fingers down to the yellow.
She had the harsh hearty laughter
Of the women who believe the men will leave them.
All the mothers I knew went nuts.
Hair the color of a screwdriver.
It's a cliché, but it's an altar.
Cotton candy spun into a knot.
Especially rich women, with art.
Kimono, muumuu.
Ice cubes.

But I was never simple. I was never simple.
The way I was raised, the men never leave a woman.
She was a woman: I could not trust her.

III. A Woman Clothed with the Sun

Imagine, all over America, women are losing bone mass.

Brittle old ladies: we create them.
Coiffured movie sirens lounging around the pool transmogrify
into brittle old sea hags.
(They don't know anything: they just nag.)
Let's let them swim out to sea.
Let's give them a spiny seahorse to ride on.
"Good-bye brittle old ladies, beautiful ones—
Ride out against the horizon and the orange sun!"

SCHADENFREUDE

If this were a movie, the sound of sizzling would foretell disaster
because you're walking out of the room leaving something
    cooking
because you have too many burners going
There should be the sound of trumpets, thin and mournful
You're going to walk into your murder.
It begins to smoke.
All the same I'm humming.
The attacker hides behind the door.
I'm whistling a happy face.
Minutes before you start shrieking, again and again
before the plaster falls down around you
before the strangulation begins
folding up clothes and putting them into drawers—your back
turned—
while the skillet, in close-up, keeps sizzling.
Minutes before the shrieking and choking.
The cupboards become lit.
Watch the doll's mouth melt.
This audience won't pity you
like big round workers who don't get pity
when they step on the bus steps in the morning and make the bus
sag momentarily. Like wizened up bodies
holding canes, heads bowed under golf hats
on their ways downtown—
This audience will laugh—
the way your eyes bulge out and your tongue is unhinged
how you return to find a kitchen filled with smoke
when we all know it's your gluttony that's caused it.
(It's the way you locked your lies up in the closet
that's led me to hate you.)

So when your doom comes—
a knife thuds into your back, let's say,
or an arrow is shot into your ribs
or a razor is pulled across your face
or you trip on a roller skate near the open cellar stairs
or you walk into a sliding glass door
or you are hung from the shower curtain rod in a plastic white
    shower
or you are stabbed with pinking shears
or demoralized with an axe handle
or beaten down the spine with a rake
or forced to swallow some golf balls
or sliced at the waist and the wounds salted
or if you merely carpet-burned your arm on the carpet
It will feel great to watch
you get it
or at least to see you experience
some slight, future, discomfort,
chagrin,
embarrassment.

THE ROLE OF THE FEMALE ARTIST
IN SOCIETY

She lives in an apartment near the freeway.
Her parents help with the rent.
She teaches part-time at junior colleges and retirement homes.
She sells a bowl here and there to the wealthier women in her
    class.
They like her and want her to be their friend.
They fix her up with men.

There are not many jobs in this economy.
She does not have a lot of clothes, a nice sofa.
There is constant struggling: e.g., the carpet is very worn.
She sells a vase, she sells a brown and red sculpture
to one of the wealthier women in her class.
They fix her up with a good "man-friend" they know.

Rembrandt is the buffer, Matisse.
Making herself willing to be like they were.
Picasso: producing a lot.
You know, reaching for the spiritual in things.
She says this to the wealthier women in her class.
They throw pots.
They fix her up "with a good-looking-guy-I-know."

You have to live in a town.
You have to live in a house.
You have to send your kids to schools.
You don't live on an airplane, drunk on miniature bottles of
    scotch,
Flying coast to coast.

FITNESS: A TRIPTYCH

1. Round Stomach, Flat Bottom

In its extreme, you will find this type at a market check-out line
in a city known for its tolerance and cruelty, its sense of humor
and its look-the-other-wayness. The woman stands waiting for
her large carton of chocolate swirl ice cream and her quart of
vodka to be bagged while she rocks back and forth on her heels,
chin thrust forward, I think she's having trouble breathing, long
beard hairs on chin and shattered pink veins strung along cheeks
and nose; hair chopped off at ears and chin, lumpy body like
potatoes under her straining blouse, she looks like she's just been
raped but she's not saying, "help!" She's not saying anything and
she does not want to look at anybody, I think. Her eyes downcast
as if the light is hurting her eyes which look as if they can barely
focus this Sunday morning as if she is in REM sleep right here
standing up like a ghost in front of me and I think it's hard for
her to even stand up at all or to be out walking around in the air
so filthy today. However sorry I feel, I am afraid.

2. Flat Stomach, Round Bottom

You'll see her while you wait at the stop light before turning the
corner, roller skating across the street in a bathing suit and
looking like she spends a lot of time outdoors: her arms and
thigh muscles tight, very visible since she wears her health to the
extreme. Is she pretty? you wonder, and you know she is, and
you know that only a man in the most high stages of love would,
sitting here next to you in a car at the stoplight, not look at her
good body go by, and admire her bottom, and would you care?
You wonder. Should you be more tolerant of men because they

like to look but staying together is something completely
different and it has nothing to do with looking at other girls,
does it? It depends: a man who yelled out the window while you
sat in the car together? But maybe looking is all right. You know
that she is good-looking but you hate to admit it but you have to
admit it, you have to admit it.

3. Here

Here perhaps there is stylish food and drink at a comfortable
roadhouse near the beach where music plays from a jukebox.
Here there is both soft and hard body shape, dancing hard to the
soft rock. But most of the women gave up drink for the sake of
their stomachs and I've noticed the growing gut, from the beer,
that the men wear on the patios and lawns around here where I
live. They are not really such Gods! Their bodies have failed
them too. In this way, the women, of which I am one, become
morally superior, designated drivers, become ladies, and the men
grown more maudlin in their beer and if they love their wives,
marriage suits them, as long as they can sit on their lawns
sometimes with another guy and look at the women going by, I
suppose that's all right. What can I do, anyway, when I'm the one
dreaming of what might have been once with that other man
who understood me so well and whose body was firmer than his
is now, the large belly I cup my arm around at night? These are
dreams doing the dishes, and the heart goes on and feels its
limits, a little warrior in a locked room.

I WAS A PHONY BALONEY!

I was a real phony baloney.
I was not a, never was a, member of the Republican party
But I was a real phony baloney.
I pretended to be meek but I was not
I pretended to be silent but I was seething
I thought I was confessional but I was teething
On my gristly, phony baloney.
I cared about my shoes (I was chattering) not really
As much as you might have thought:
Oh, sure I was (fill in the blank) and I was (fill in this spot)
But I was a real phony baloney.
I was thinking of how to overthrow the power plot
While I pretended to tend to my petty thoughts
My eyes were narrowing into harmful harmless slots
I took it out on (Blank) and (Her name I forgot)
I was a real phony baloney.
I pretended to be meek but I was not
I pretended to be weak but I was a block
of solid phony baloney.

Envoi:
I pretended to be sighing but I was enjoying my lot:
I was a sorry, sorry. (Baloney.)

MARRIAGE

One day my husband came home with a jar of generic peanut
    butter.
He used it for the mousetraps.
One, two, three, they were dead.
One squealed as his fur was pulled off into the glue.
He threw him into the sewer only half-dead.
The day before he had been running.
Hopping out of the trash can onto my foot.
Running along the edge of the closet.
Another: four. Another: five. Another: six.

I said I would make peanut butter cookies.
He said, are you going to use that generic peanut butter? Gross.
He did not want the cookies.
He said, I don't even like peanut butter cookies.
I said, you told me you liked them.
He said, I don't remember.

Not remembering!
As it went on, I actually stomped my foot.
Not remembering what he says!
He was taking off his tie. He was hanging up his shirt.
He says, you need to be more strong.
He doesn't know that this will never make sense to me.
I'm not interested in being strong, as he is not interested in
    remembering.

ALLEGORY OF THE SUPERMARKET

Procession of death,
Day-Glo death,
Potato death,
Death of strawberry.
Death strapped into a handi-six-pack
Death in vodka, scotch, the vitamin-fortified cigarette cough.
Juice of cow in a box,
Broccoli piled up man-felled trees
How long have I been in here?
Our faces look left, right, slow, so slow, so sleepy
We reach for the non-fat,
The boxes of breadsticks, the round glue of pregnancy.
No one ever says, really, anything.
Plastic bags from the roll rippp
Let's grab a lettuce from the stacks of lettuce,
Bee in the bonnet on the label of the jar of honey,
Darling: the non-world-yellow cheese,
the price,
the size chosen by a stranger's desire,
for my teeth.
Box of food for the pet at home, standing in our kitchen.
The shelves of canned fruit, yellow bullets of mustard jars
The piles of onions, the dusty garlic piles,
The triangular figure of tomatoes,
The baskets we lay our deaths down in
Fetching cans of halos.
Cry into your toilet paper,
your spray starch,
your light bulbs and lobsters in tanks near the cashier's booth
their claws held together by rubber bands
Cry into that water

Fish belly up on the Styrofoam surfaces
in refrigeration
headless feetless chickens
Turkeys across the aisle, look-alike big bodies, frozen.
Shelves of bread loaves like big leather shoes of sad old clerks
not like
smell of yeast and life's
an open wound, festering, and a feast of fools.
No dignity, my darling,
in these last three hours of the world.

II
Cataract Surgery

PARTS OF THE EYE

My father and I dissected pigs' eyes at our dining room table
which we covered with ripped bedsheets, then newspapers

• • •

(A lot of times I unplug my phone . . . I think someone's going
to call and say, "Dad's dead". . . I'm afraid of hearing it . . . I'm
afraid of it because more than anything I guess I'd be . . . you
know . . .)

• • •

He ordered the eyes from a slaughterhouse and brought them
    home
in a jar of formaldehyde. He brought home surgical tools: a
    scalpel
for me, one for him, tweezers, tiny scissors.

• • •

(. . . it's confusing . . . the money issue . . . I mean I'm so guilty
now . . . sometimes I think . . . though maybe . . . I don't know)

• • •

I imitated his movements. First: *incision.*
He traced the scalpel around the cornea's perimeter at the iris'
edge; he pulled the cornea up and out: Wet. This is the first step
he explained, and one must not make a mistake.

• • •

(. . . he sued his brother . . . they had a jury trial that lasted all one
summer . . . supposedly his brother was all alcoholic and bloated
. . . I never went to the courtroom . . . I guess it was less about
the forgery and fraud, the will and the money than about my
uncle's . . . there was testimony from the maids and houseboy
about the noises and the people who hung around . . . he was
basically married to another man for thirty years . . . they drank
vodka—like a quart a day—and bought lobsters all the time . . .
this was the thing they talked about . . . finally my uncle fell down
in a hospital room in the middle of the night . . . nobody found
him till the next day . . .)

• • •

We popped the lens out. Small, thick, tough. We cut around
the iris: just a narrow film of brown—
He extracted it whole: a circle.
The pupil is just a hole that changes with the light, he explained,
but it does not exist in itself.

• • •

(Anyway, before my dad fell down on the tennis court and all
that, I knew something was going to happen. I *knew*. I thought
about it all summer, I can remember walking down Mass. Ave.
and thinking about it, writing about it in my journal: something's
going to happen)

• • •

The stub on the back of the eyeball is the optic nerve
which connects the eye to the brain of the pig.
My dad picked up the eyeball and squeezed out the *vitreous humor*.
I said, "It looks like snot." The retina covers
the back wall of the eye. We couldn't remove it.

(. . . to think of him lying there in his hospital room with tubes in
his nose, chest, dick . . . I kept getting the chills . . . he and my
brother laughed about walking down hospital halls with your IV
behind you, my brother had to have his colon removed . . .
sometimes you wish . . . I don't know . . .)

I placed each part of the eye on a posterboard glued to wood
Then, printing carefully, labeled each with its name.
I brought it to my class the next day and explained
each part of the eye and how it works.

THE SLOW HOURS

As a kid, I was a diver for pearls,
my hair floating over the water's edge.
I didn't— and nothing around me—
Flowers sang, far away in the pond.

I wanted to know if I could scream underwater—
I tried. I tried to bloom with noise in the bath
water. It never worked, just like it didn't taste right
when I mixed together a glass of milk, and one of water—

though I tried it every day at lunch. In the outside,
I carried a basket and collected the spoiled grapefruit
from under the trees. With my thousand cats and dogs
I led a journey to the forest in the back of the yard where

I kept my treehouse, and my tire on a tree. There
my legion and I lay face down in the damp.
I fingered among the fronds for a four-leaf clover.
Hours and hours passed.

My best friend used to draw fine line pencil drawings of rats and build tall stick and circle structures on his desk when I sat in front of him and would turn around. Even though I tried to be a boy and play as well as they did when I shaved my legs at the end of the year they all noticed when my kneesock fell down and then they shut up. The next year in junior high my sister and I bought a magazine with men laid out like women were in *Playboy* but they were kind of old looking and ugly lying on a leather couch or something with a drink with ice in it laughing leaning over to move a chess piece on the table with legs slightly open and showing it even then I had no idea of erection or masturbation except that it was okay to do it not to be ashamed and not to be afraid of menstruation when it came though I knew from my sisters how the cramps hurt it felt exactly like I thought it would, like I had been preparing for it all of my twelfth year. We drove on the freeway and I prayed to God I would get it I don't know why it was not a good thing no one wanted it everyone hated it it made you kind of weird I didn't realize the way I lay on the bed and thought about men putting blindfolds on me might be part of it: three years later I knew it was not at all like their putting a finger inside of you: just the way they had to put their whole body on top of you it was really surprising how it tore you open how my skin was ripping my whole insides I thought in the dark there I would have a nervous breakdown what in the world was this thing we couldn't finish. It took me several months before he was able to come like normal and I understood. Three years before when I was with my best friend in the garage why they wanted me to put my hand down his swim trunks before we rode our bikes around I wouldn't go very far or move my fingers though I took off my shorts and pulled my bathing suit bottoms down and then back up so they

could see it I understood why we were doing that and why I took
my shirt off and untied my bathing suit top so they could stand
five feet away from me and look and why after that we talked on
the telephone almost every night and I liked to imagine myself in
his yard in the treehouse he told me about.

THE KID FROM THE COMMUNE

In the commune he slept
among the pillows, on a mattress,
on top of a sleeping bag unzipped (a dog had pissed on it)
under a bedspread from Mom's Mom's garage
(an acrylic imitation of the patchwork quilt of some grandma)
Indian tapestry fabric sewn into a pillow he lay his head on
(Mom bought it by the yard at a store called The the)
She stitched it around some foam rubber, and voilà.
His mom sewed Indian tapestry into dresses—short maternity
    shape, with angel sleeves—
She picked it out of a pattern book, at the yardage store.

His mom had nursed him under a tree,
under the stars,
under the moon,
seen through the pop-up top in the Volkswagen camper
(It was expensive, but the dad had had some money then)
It was like an illustrated story book.
He never wore diapers—believe it—it was against the religion
they had turned to, the mom and dad—
the religion where they gave up their money, heart, clothes, car,
    and kid.
He was raised by the mothers in the group.
The mothers! All the men were men All the women were cooks
    maids
indifferent blissed faces
of oneness.

Baking bread was sacred. Childbirth, the social occasion.
They didn't drink wine. But occasionally they did.
The moms and dads slept with others then:

What is love but something to share with everyone? or
    something like this.
It's good to dance under the trees.
The August heat is like a relief:
Open your heart let go of your past!
The men with their smiling mouths above their beards
See how gentle they're being. Some even like sewing and baking.
And they will leave with a woman and kids: go back to the city.

Our boy gets up from his bed, goes to the public school.
The moms and dads stay home repairing bus engines and baking
    and hoeing
the growing garden. The business of selling jams was beginning.
Sarah Ann went to the towns and sold it in her straight clothing.
She never went to live in the city. She stayed and stayed and
    stayed.

Our boy was laughed at by the others—
rich kids with clean pants and hair washed and brushed daily.
Moms who looked twice as old as his mom.
He could not read.
He was not very smart, our boy.
He wore his hair too long and wore a peace sign strung on a
    leather thong around his neck.
What a weirdo!
No one played with our boy.
The best he could hope for was for the type of family who are
    professional pitiers

to pity him, to take him in in the afternoons to play
in a fully equipped play room—
but not in those days.
When the mother picks him up from school (the blissed smile
    the angel sleeves
the lank brown hair she will wear into eternity—)

She thinks that while
her own parents wondered aloud,
"Where did we go wrong? Was it something we did?"
She never will. She will never wonder this.
And she never did.

CATARACT SURGERY

On Saturdays
after English Breakfast tea, dry rye toast
and one vitamin
you'd set the sports page aside and start working.
One morning
I slumped down across from you, said, hi.

You said, hi.
I said, what are you writing?
You said, oh, this thing about hmmhmm, cataract surgery.
Oh.
Interocular lenses. Oh yeah, I said, I remember
those people in your office with the stitches
right in their eyeballs! You said,
exactly. It's quite amazing what it's doing. Don't you
love this room in the rain? You said, and lifted
your shoulders up, then down. We looked
at the water pitting the windows.
White caps floated by in the channel.

In the kitchen by the oven door (later)
you scuffled the floor and waved your arms in the air and said
woo hoo I love baked potatoes!
I said, I think dinner is almost ready so maybe
you'd better move that stuff from the table. I said,
are you still working on the thing about the cataracts?
No, a letter about the airport, you said. I said, good.
You said, well, it's getting worse. You put your hand
to your chest and said, *God,* I *love* this *room* in the *rain!*
It's like you're floating . . . it's like you're in a shower!
I said, I like to read in the shower but everything gets wet.

With Mom and candles
all three of us back at the workspot
you stuck your spoon into pea soup and tasted and said
Oh this is good! Just how I like it! Real hot!
You broke the loaf. You said, this is the *best bread, where*
in the world did it come from? I said, you know where—
why do you act like you don't? It's from the bakery by
the post office. You said, Oh.

THE LOST COAST, CALIFORNIA

These people left. They disappeared from our shores, down south.
The women never look like whores
Never the compromised, damaged nose-job self.
They are helpful, and when I look into their eyes
When I purchase a linen skirt,
They try to look inside. But more afraid than kind.
Stoned Dads, opening the supermarket freezer door.
Baby in the shopping cart, a tie-dyed romper on.
A couple of teenagers beside him—why so quiet everyone?
I don't like it.
"Nature Bats Last" the bumper sticker threatens
Out in the parking lot. But I don't get it.
It took me several days, not just a minute.
The road leads to the stream with abandoned wrecks
Trailers set aside the dry trees and they're old trailers
The trees, of course, are famous for being ancient trees.
I'm sure I would get it, if I listened.
The terrain is dangerous and the road we're on winds up and up,
A steep incline
Trees that would eat you up
Soak you back into the earth—
The environmentalist guerrilla died in her cabin back there,
    last year
We passed the place, someplace we drove by.
We wouldn't think of trying to find someone like her.

When I was growing up the surfers of a certain kind
called our town Zooport or Zoopit (Newport)
What did I know? It was really some kind of paradise
I was a kid   riding the bus through countryside
Eucalyptus trees and hawks   dry brown hills to the sea   glass
    business offices next

Then wide freeways, sprinklered lawns.
It changed from the country into the city.
Some people were sad   Many were too busy   Many were
    making it happen.
Those stoned boys went to Maui or Eureka or Washington
"I saw Hanford   I saw John"
You'd hear every once in a while about someone
A stoned or alky surfer long gone;
My brother's friend said, "I want to feel like I matter
    somewhere—a small town"
He went North
He went to Eureka Shasta Oregon
All those people gone
The hometown a completely different place—
Now you can shop like you're in Paris, New York, Milan.
It's like that: rich and fun.
The women look like whores, the men look strong.

So I vacationed on the Lost Coast
What did they find here, I wanted to know.
What had we lost?
I saw that: vines can grow so thick and tough they can hug a
    house right back.
It's hard to make a living unless you're really rich or used to
    being broke.
The crumbling highway could fall beneath us.
Salt spray on ocean rock delicate spring flower in a field
    under fog—
A natural food store named "The Corners of the Mouth"
Providing Nourishment. It's beautiful there—
Caution cones   the road *is* falling off the cliff.
"Nature Bats Last."
We drove all the way up, but we went all the way back.

NO, NO, NOSTALGIA!

I thought I'd end up a Hippie American Gothic
Those people who nod their heads and listen carefully
And hug one another from arms inside of overalls
Round eyes in round glasses
But I never liked the kitchens they had
Overrun with jars full of saved things
And bins full of grains gotten from bins full of grains
which were gotten on all-day-long shopping-expedition-type
    shopping trips.
The car, the van rode very slow . . .
But I liked the long-haired women who kneaded bread
and calmly carried their bodies to the beach where they stripped
their clothes off unselfconsciously, and swam.
You know, bearded men and Viet Nam and all that . . .
But they were very stern with me when I didn't understand
soldiers and helicopters and the *meaning* of long hair and of
mind expansion.
This was the world of my older siblings
They were my parent-surrogates, said I,
after a few months of my Jungian-oriented therapy.
Three hippie sisters who were mothers.
(Aha.) The other parents were mostly on a fabulous vacation
    to France
So I had to hate it, and I had to like it later and I had to hate it.
I had to throw up at the sight of sprouts,
and the elixirs measured out in eyedroppers,
and the sea salt and the paperbacks about cancer as a Tri-Lateral
    Commission plot,
and the water distiller which ran all night long.
(If my brother-in-law lay on the couch all day and smoked pot,
wasn't he merely lazy?)

Grant Wood got it right: those faces
American toughness and humorless virtue are all right
It's the judgmental part I can do without
The way they raise the kids: everyone greeted with
a vision of wholesomeness, with suspicious mouths.

III

Marginalia

I'm driving a fast car out of control.
Frustrating, how they lose.
Their life was one big dunno.
Failure. Failure. A drum roll.
They raise rabbits or live with a girl or get a career in electronics.
The clock ticks.
They had a friend until the friend split.
Their parents loved them, the books gather.
The clock ticks.
The child must drive his car too fast from this disaster, to a ditch.
Must outdrive the police into the orchard, where the body's hit.
Must fall from the dance marathon into the gutter.
Those dreams where you run and run and run and run and run
    and run.

They will fade away from the lover.
They will rise and lift the tire iron,
will promise and promise the jailer,
will dig out of the administration,
will take the shot in the arm again,
will exchange the dollar for the secrets of sin,
will find themselves at the edge of moonlit water.

Until the law embraces them,
soothes them down like a mother,
carries them to safety.
Each day the sun shines steadily, no more than is necessary.

You know, we looked at, touched carefully, and studied a copy of Erasmus' *Praise of Folly* with marginal drawings by a young Holbein. I gave the seminar an analysis of Holbein's early woodcuts, made around the same time as the marginal drawings. I knew Holbein as a young man, I thought. A different man than the one who painted "The Ambassadors," a mature artist so aware of the complexity of his craft, I said. The marginalia included a friar wearing an ass' head while giving a sermon. In pen and ink, yet! They were, I noted, "small, personal, intimate, and funny." Folly is pictured as a woman with visible and nicely proportioned breasts. (Remember the great marginalia in MAD magazine?)

Then, my brain felt clear like whiteness, glass, snow fields. I felt adrenaline surges. I never had to leave the Library. I loved the travel books with tiny foldout maps of the sixteenth-century sea. I compared them to the first edition of *Gulliver's Travels*. I really loved that closed quiet. Around rare books you can only write in pencil. Finally, though, I'd had enough when I finished my degree. You know, at a Christmas party a year after this time I joked, "It was like I was in the Brain Olympics." I said, "I could be a good amateur but never a professional." Then my brother spoke in reply.

Still, I knew how to browbeat the others. I knew how to outargue the point. I knew how to see the meaning of nudity in the marginalia in the late editions of Books of Hours. Women in tubs with fashionable distended stomachs surrounding the prayers. My professor was often astonished at my leaps between ideas; she was a very nice woman who wanted me to get a Ph.D. I talked a lot about Erasmus because I was the only one who'd read him. I was the kind of person people make fun of.

So, I was reading this *Ripley's Believe It or Not!* book in the bathroom at my work. I work in a public library. I read a little morality tale about objects swept off to sea: they mean nothing, therefore. Objects die too. You can't believe in them. When I imagine myself in a future war, I always think of myself as being one of those people who will be useless in the new society: arcane knowledge about manuscripts, and typesetting, indeed! I'll be one of the first to be killed if this happens.

Because, I am very far away from someone with hungry, American immigrant needs. My family is now decadent. We're serving the purpose of useless details. Did I have a certain purpose? A dignity? All those things revolutionaries don't need. Revolutionaries don't need toy stores. Revolutionaries don't need me. Would I plead, *I never harmed anyone!* I did, of course. Most of all, I would have harmed the soldier whose job it was to kill me.

KITSCH

A canvas, 11" by 14",
amber, yellow, and brown: fall leaves.
Two deer painted on top of the leaves.
They don't stand on the ground: there's no dirt and no trees.
A mother deer with round black eyes, discernible eyelashes
and a slight smile
leans down to her baby whose face matches, whose eyes
    return: *love.*
A discernible Sunday breeze.
One artist's work, hung on pegboard, for me to see.
I have left my clothes in the dryers of Bud's Suds.
SIDEWALK ART SALE TODAY! I'm taking a stroll.
Down the street you can buy photographs of carousel horses:
the heads thrown back, the teeth. For what reason?
The deer's bodies are spotted with paint.
I keep staring. Down the street
a clown in a baggy white suit, a head of day-glo
will hand you a balloon. THANKS FOR COMING!
The little deer gazes into the mother's eyes.
They say nothing of the sadness, except to say: *it's touching.*

Are roller coasters a valid interpretation of fear?
—I can smell it here—
This street is a street of fear
All that love enclosing itself away:
We love mothers and children and deer.

I remember how we stood at attention
feeling a love we couldn't give a home
like the lost puppy I cried for.

I cried for the sheep in cartoons
threatened by the wolf. Arms given over
to wailing. I ran through a house, screaming,
"Don't let him don't let him do it!"

AESTHETIC QUESTIONS

What's the woman doing in the garden with a hoe?
What's the woman doing breaking the ground with a hoe in
    the garden?
What's the garden doing with a woman in it breaking its ground
    with a hoe?
What's the poem doing in a garden where the woman is breaking
    its ground with a hoe?

What is she wearing? (She's nude.)
What is she planting? (Old shoes.)
What does the garden represent? (Hey you.)

Now a man comes into the garden where the woman breaks the
    ground with a hoe
to plant shoes. The man is a man and a) all men are mortal b)
    Aristotle is a man so
c) what will the man do before he dies? He dies at the end of the
    poem, you know.

He brings her more shoes? (No.)
He brings her fertilizer and water? (I'm sorry. No.)
He brings a picnic of bread and wine because she is "thou" and
    they have a picnic
in the breeze on the grass by the garden.
Are you saying this is *Dejeuner sur L'Herbe?*

No, I'm not saying that at all. (Just exactly what are you saying.)

IT TOOK A VILLAGE

43

Every village has its village idiot.
Its Frankenstein, the monster, and the mob.

Fakelore, faxlore, bumper sticker wisdom.
I hope your own mom and dad tried to love you more.

THE NEIGHBORHOOD
OF SUCCESSFUL MARRIAGE

In the neighborhood where I grew up, the men
Shone like the shields of warriors and they did everything.
The women hid
As they grew older they became smaller, creating
Gargantuan and antiquely gorgeous bedrooms,
Sometimes left their bodies totally,
Until, finally, small, wrinkled, smiling, you see them walking
In the evenings along the beach sidewalk at sunset
(It is a paradise, isn't it?)
Always in the company of the husband,
The woman's ears open, her eyes straight ahead-down,
As the man is talking talking talking.
He is full of ideas
He is full of life
He is full of rage
He is full of discipline
He provides.

When she stops to say hello to the neighbors—old man, old
    woman, grandson—,
(Teaching the meaning of paradise, passing it on)
The men smile,
But the men tense up.
Their chests are lifted, strong.
They nod. *Hurry. Hurry up.*

She's pretty if you *think* about it, if you let your eyes go
if you put away your vision of hair blowing, turning in wind-
     machine wind
with eyes closed hugging herself: make it her:
The tiny red bow attached to her red bra which peeks out from
     her linen blouse
—they're ripe breasts, after all—is evocative if you *feel* your way
You can see how it *would be attractive*
(some men), you think, sure.
Her slow, slow gait is not subtle. Bovine legs, lips.
A painter would want to paint you, someone says to her.
Her curves, yes, are mountainous. Out of style, nonetheless.

Her fashion is fat fashion, let's face it.
Large in a fur coat: Masoch's fate, Sade's wisdom.
It's only pastel, pastime, part-time sensual, let's face it.
Don't ever let's see it.
Her face is a fat face in a chocolate bar, let's face it.
No one hugs her around the hips and places his face in her ur—
let's face it. She's no one's ur-lover except in

reflection, let's face it. Amazon walking purposelessly looking
purposeful, let's face it. Her cosmetic comedy inflicted into
     her skin
is depressing, let's face it. Her comedy, which is tragedy,
is driving no one wild, let's face it. If you think about her if
     you think
about her which you do only if she's facing you across
the spaghetti dinner you ordered lonely together on your evening
away from a real life, she has no backbone.
She has a life, if you think about it.

If you feel your way into it, she's attractive, but you would never
touch it, it's too complicated, all that wanting not wanting
wanting not wanting is the way you think she feels it.
Those arms around her hips: it isn't for you, it isn't for her. What
    was it

the art critic you heard said about past portraits of naked fleshy
    women: they had strength, power—
he said. But, who, today, believes it?

47

is an epoxy glue for lovers
trying to win a gold star for their good job

a common cause for outcasts
remembering to write the wrong.

A calculated chorus to cicadas
counting the choral curves

of coral, in the sea. Angels, lithe. Mistresses
swooning in bloom

Palpitations late at night. The stillest birth.
Let me tell you

about a man: he was. He was.

INTERVIEW WITH AN ALCHEMIST
IN THE NEW AGE

Someone, if you pay the price, can hypnotize you
and you can speak, from memory, oh so long ago embedded into
    your soul,
about the past, and history, and your place in it, how
    you struggled
in the heat and the dust near the Great Pyramid of Giza,
how you gazed into the mirror of your beloved,
how you took a bow with your fellow thespians, in Greece,
how a sycophant betrayed you in the Hall of Mirrors, at
    Versailles,
how he kissed you before the duel where he was murdered
    for you
—in the country somewhere, in the South—
and you were forced to marry the victor. Or
how you didn't starve during the famine that killed your child,
that's the source of the nagging pain in your side,
and you can feel—it's still very real—the leeches placed on
    your chest
though of course with these primitive mechanisms of medicine,
you bled to death. Is this why
you fear the scalpel so?
Were you cauterized by a tribal-rite clitorectomy?
Were you a castrato?
When your teeth rotted in Spain in the seventeenth century,
what had you done that was remiss?
Where does it now fit?
Was, perhaps, the Armada involved?

Because it's yours, it's your Karma, buddy, it's *your problem*
It's *your* history, and history is your problem.

It's your responsibility, now,
to change the tire on your neighbor's car
because you once beheaded him because he once beat you at a
    game of chess
when you were the King of France, when you were ruthless.
And now you're not ruthless: see, there's a kind of symmetry
    involved.
Just think,
Albert Einstein may already have come back,
maybe he's a kid,
maybe he's in the womb and about to be born.
Maybe he'll arrive by spaceship.
These are extraordinary times, of course—that's why.
Have we ever felt the tenor of the spiritual with such
    force before?
Is this not the end of time?
Oh, I don't know. It's weird, all right, and it's kind of neat
to bear the children while wearing a costume from the
    Middle Ages,
to wait for the Pony Express to ride into town,
to be the shaman for the Eskimos,
to be the butler for Henry Ford!
George Washington's dentist—where is he now!
History, after all, doesn't belong to Cinderella, or to Henry VIII,
or to Jesus—perhaps you wiped his forehead before the
    Crucifixion—
Who knows?
Well, wouldn't it be fun to think about?
And it might help you work out the problem you're having with
    your father
Or with the guy at the 7–11 who constantly berates you,
who once even hurled a doughnut at you—
(You rowed together in a ship just like in "Ben-Hur")

Anyhow, who does it harm

(since you were once Mozart, send in the harpsichord
    music now)
if you pay to be hypnotized and to find out
how karmic or unkarmic you are?
Oh no, it's not just kidding around, really—
You'll never know for sure if you were really a monk once,
but if you were—well, wow.

IV
No Longer a Girl

The city was a gray city.
I was dreaming of nothing then.
I had no hopes of love anymore.
My back was breaking.
My heart was cracked.
Though it wasn't broken by another person.
I liked to shout, but there was no one to listen.
I was no longer a girl: no one looked and they once did.
It was dark but there were no storms to create verdant forests.
Drizzle, steady, on the train which ran down the freeway, then
    went underground.
I remember those guys nodding out, that kid playing with
    himself
All the way home from the airport. In the cute house I rented
There was this stain on the planked floor which trailed
directly from the bathroom to the around-the-corner
    bedroom door.
Someone had walked that path, dripping wet, for years.
I wasn't doing it, I swear.
It's hard to believe, but there was a crematorium on the corner.
Really. And there was a graveyard where my street dead-ended.
I found the graves of the Civil War soldiers, marked by cannons.
There were ponds, bent trees, and leaves floating in the waters.
And if you walked to the top of the hill
You could see Merritt Lake downtown.
You could see the Pacific beyond.
You could see light shimmer on the water but everything
Inside of me held still.
Not afraid of the feel of the dead,
Not afraid of the living sitting in cafés or walking the dog:
On Sundays I'd walk down to the street near my house

Where there were stores and things to do, even a movie theater,
Because I thought: "I'll take a walk and that will be fun"
But everything was sad, even the joy I once felt opening the big
Sunday newspaper was gone.
After a while I left that city, when I was done.

UNFASTEN, LIFT UP

I could have opened your shirt like unwrapping a present and
here I would find all the jealousy I need and I am sure the way
you would wrap yourself around me would be uncomfortable to
the point where it almost takes a ghost's shape I'm sure it would
be but I don't like imagining your face how fierce it would
become when you'd arrive on top of me though maybe I have
you all wrong I know that just for touching me you would be
very worried about every move I made just like it wasn't very
good how the man in the pastry shop asked me to taste the
chocolate mousse cake it made you stop talking until I cheered
you up yes I like doing that for you and bringing you your plate
in any cafeteria where we were and how I'd bring you silverware
and ask what else you might like you'd ask and not even seem
apologetic about it which turned me on and I'd take care of your
coat for you it was winter worry about your mood please watch
what I do attend to each change in your whine it would always be
this way wouldn't it your jealousy like some divine diamond I'd
wear on my hand for you like a weight of sadness and darkness
between us as you know because I defined this to you one day
you'd know how I like the idea of my body under someone's It
might be yours though I am not sure what I would have done if
after I'd stopped rubbing your back as we lay on your bed just
like any other kinds of girlfriends what we would have done if
we'd gone on with this present: each button on your shirt to
unfasten and my skirt which you lift up.

My scissors cut the tape which is taping up the boxes I'm
    sending
Scissors from my eighth grade sewing class.
My first initial and surname painted on them in red nail polish.
They'll be among the last artifacts I pack.
Boogaloo, honey, boogaloo, boogaloo.
Mailing the boxes to the new house,
which is the old house.
Inside my chest is a harp which is twisted in two:
Shribblypibblebitcrimyshitsuckercocksuckerfuck.

Tape makes a noise like screeching when it's pulled from
    its wheel.
It's so loud in this furnitureless room
I bet the man next door, right behind the wall, can hear.
One night he invited me over and I brought a six-pack of beer.
He said, "I want your body"
It was flattering, sort of, as I know I am prettier than his wife.
It felt like we were in a room the door of which is ajar
A hotel where the rooms are filled with a wail.
It felt flattering like those scenes that run through my mind . . .

I address these boxes to my parents, to whose house they go.
I used to think sex would be great while tears ran down
    my cheeks
and my chest heaved as I sobbed for any old reason at all.
Then it happened. All that week I had cried.
He said, *it makes you seem more real.*
It looked so much more enchanting

when I saw it last year in a scene in a movie:
It was as if that director knew me
the actor undressed her ruthlessly while she lay on the bed
    in tears.

SHAMANS

We were high on our dopamine and norephenedrine
Looking for the endorphin afterblast,
The serotonin afterglow.
Why was that?
The brain chemistry was slow,
So we revved up on coffee, cigarettes, alcohol, the sound of our
   own voices
And we fell into the groove of good listening-eye contact.
Adjudicating music with melancholy undertones.
We welcomed our respective hallucinations,
Mine, I described them, were sitting in the outer office where I
   worked, were ghosts.
Someone else, her room spun and she never slept.
Teacups flew around the ceiling—
—Like a ride at Disneyland—I reminded her, though she had
   never seen Disneyland.
That was what I had seen on the ceiling as a child,
So I knew teacups were nothing to sneer at.
She nodded sagely, anyway, as this was the nature of our
   conversations.
They were stupid conversations.
We made out and kissed people, rolled around on the grass,
   came down
Alone in our rented apartments. For me that was full of fear, like
   this:
A feeling like someone is tapping me on the shoulder to wake
   me up.
My back to the door or about to fall asleep: that tap.
But I lived alone,
So I was just creating a spirit-companion.
It was very dark the evening I decided I would just let go, see
   how far into the end I could take myself.

The others, the ones I had talked to, were gone now.
We had scattered from the sacred place where we had found
    each other.
Now we were into our ministries.
So there I was, saying, *take me*
The night darkening Pleasant Valley Road,
The street I lived off of. I could see down it forever. So
I waited for dark crows, or dark death, whatever . . .
But I woke up the next day.
The veins inside my forehead pounded
The cramps inside my belly laid it on.
And that was it.
Oh sure, I was changed.
Oh sure, I had fulfilled my tasks.
Yes, I was given the gift to see things,
And yes, when I saw them, I was stupefied with fear and wonder.

THE FOURTH OF JULY

The guy leading the game calls out, "Okay, red's turn!"
which is me, standing in the weeds.
I laugh at myself sheepishly.
The girl ahead of me kisses her boyfriend easily.
Between turns, they hug each other, unashamed.
I wish it were me.
I hit the ball nearer to the metal hoop: it goes through.
Everyone's nice to me, even though I'm last at croquet.
"Okay, orange, then green," he yells, he smiles,
and his boy runs around and around in a circle.
A husband and wife now take turns: yellow, then blue.
The kids bang their mallets together to make noise.
I can smell the barbecue going.
Dusk starts coming into the sky.

This is the first party I've been to in a while.
My friend that I've known since seventh grade invited me.
This is the first holiday since I'm not drinking.
I'm thankful I have a friend. At the end of the party
My friend, her husband and I go up to the balcony and play
    Scrabble.
Fireworks go off from the dune nearby.
We can hear them crack, explode.
Everything feels nice and cozy, though.
When I think about drinking, I let it go.
When the game's over, I say, Thanks! Goodbye!
Do you remember that "X" song?—the singer, John Doe,
    lamenting,
"Hey, baby, it's the Fourth of July"—
It plays on the radio in my car.
The poor woman in the song

can't do anything but sit alone in the dark, and her boyfriend
wants her to come out and love him, but she won't.
It hurts too much, so I turn it off.

A car's windshield lies all over the road.
The collision is skidded sideways.
The police wave the cars around the accident with flashlights.
They wave me by, and I look, but I don't see a body.
I drive slowly through the flares on the asphalt, then keep going.
On the other side of the highway, an ambulance is coming.

FIVE SKETCHES, IN A RESTAURANT

1.

She's stranded on her own planet
is my fifty-word treatment of it.
She could not live in any place where it ever snowed she's having
a power-dinner late with an acquaintance she's trying to woo
Phone call, excuse me—
Briefcase list, excuse me—
Her clients insist—
Woo to her way of closing deals in Denver, Dallas—
(Hand cupped over the receiver)
What I'm thinking of—excuse me—
In a nutshell: the bottom line is: hands clasped together
Very, very, very
charming, well-shod, and well-to-do.

2.

Lopped off hair and cable-knit sweater, it's okay if she lives
in snow or really any weather for:
No, no, really—it's okay—!
For, she's for real, she's a flannel nightie
She's a trooper she's a champion she's a cookie
She's a greeting card paying homage to her smile-filled
Pansy-arranging
arithmetic audiotapes counting piemaking
ribbon bow tying package place-card table setting etcetera many
    many
(strike up the band)
Children, Many *many!*

3.

Miss America
standing at the end of the runway, the magic carpet
Here, Mr. The-Business-of-America-is-to-make-a-fortune,
Here she is.
Do it.
A sacrifice.
Do it.
Do it.
Do it twice.
Love her: your bride price.

4.

She's not a ship
or a logo
Do not
Honor her image
Denounce those men who made it
Make sure you put her in a lot of bra ads so that we can get
    really, really angry
Worship the Goddess alone
If you're called a __________(for any of it), repeat the litany
about society needing to change first *Society! Inadequate* childcare!
(Though you would never care to *have* children, you respect those
    who do)
It's a fashionable tangent to wander off to—
No, it's not really funny. I'm sorry
To make fun of you, who are *really trying.*
I know how hard it is, since your mother betrayed you.

5.

O Clare Booth Luce,
O Mary McCarthy,
O Cold Un-Self-Destructing
Athena with her rosy-fingered dawn
Medusa exists in the reflection of her shield—only—
Distant relations, were they? More like
Sisters who never spoke.
I see my face in the clean, clean white dinner plate.
Which face in the clean, clean white dinner plate?

ARRANGEMENT IN DARK AND LIGHT

You can ramble around the house without turning the light on.
Because you know your way around in the dark better than you
    think, really.
And the moon will shine inside the tipped shutters, the
    streetlamp provides.
You can hear cars drive past, once in a while.
You may hear a cricket sing a song.
Sometimes you will tend to the wound that opens at your
    breastbone.
If you breathe into it, pain feels like fire.
You can stay here a long while.
Sleep comes when it's nearly morning, when the earliest morning
    news shows have come on,
And you've put on the TV because you're tired of yourself.
Someone talk, please. And then you sleep.
Later you have the day, no night, no fear, the light.
This is the way you walk through it.
You get in the car; You don't miss your exits.

Inside your wound you hold a cage
With a bird locked up inside it,
A bird you took away from the river
Where you left your seeds in the rich damp soil
You thrust each one down into the dark dirt
And said, *please grow this time, please grow for me*
Though the river is sick, full of plastic six-pack rings,
The usual rusting beach chair, damp cardboard, rigid bottles,
An overturned shopping cart (water trickling through the metal);
But the dirt seemed ready,
And the bird was real. The bird scavenging for anything to eat,
    saying,

Life,
fire,
saga,
the energy of a child.
Flapping wings, taking flight—
A medicine you craved for the time of darkening of the light.

CALIFORNIA

They are hot weather.
All the family birthdays are in the summer.
—the inflatable pool on the cement slab
—the closely razored heads
—the flannel shirts and jeans to "grow into"
for the winter season but it's sunny, and hot, forever,
the house had no landscaping
In the desert—
He stands with his brother near the walls of the house in the
    desert.
In that town on the endless highway.

I imagine this family history from the photographs,
Scattered inside this drawer and that, stuffed into shoeboxes
Not neatly arranged into albums, as mine would be—
Not composed in any particular way—
Taking in too many vast, empty spaces.
The faces: relentlessly cheerful, or blurred.
How do people come to have no past, no illustrious ancestors,
    anyway?
(Like me, like me, like I do!)

The town is off a highway people drive to get to the ski places.
They pass the town right by.
There is dirt and more dirt and cactuses.
My father, who owns a lot of real estate,
Owns some of these desert places—
The land is worth nothing.
(My family was rich and we lived on the beaches.)

We drove to the ski place, so we turned off to see the town.

This is my husband now.
Dusty, old, some discount stores, some houses
Cordoned off with wire fences.
More dirt and more highways around, till you've left it.
But he said it was a good place for a boy to grow up.
Lizards to catch, and land to run around on . . .
Relentlessly cheerful,
Telling me as we drove
Through it once, and moved on.
And it was
Nice and quiet: all that land stretching nowhere, just the sound
    of wind, for miles—

"A man can hear himself think here," is I think how they say it.

THE ZEITGEIST

It's time to fall into the arms of God.
The century's ending, the meter's running.
All those we *communicated* so deeply with
didn't listen. Their mirrors
were as thick with toothpaste advertising as ours were.
We didn't hear, did we? *Maybe God hears*
It's private, this serious world,
confession and repentance and seeding the earth,
but you might want to wear a crucifix around your neck
as a lot of people do seem to worship the devil, for real,
We can fear each other's dance steps,
each man will molest a child, each woman will shout down
her child, each teenager will draw a pentagram for suicide
each counselor will tell us how, how—.

Perhaps this is the fear they predicted in the novels I liked a lot:
Totalitarian fear, the fear that would chain us
as a real war was played for pretend reasons.
No more spirits, not more grog, the spirits are too much with us
They walk through our halls: if you look you can't miss them.
White dress shirts on hangers I've seen them float down
Their expressions are blank so full of rage dead dead eye sockets
Blank as skulls on gravestones. Flies fly around
the dead animals who die under construction cranes.
The older generation is passing away,
the little garden we live in each of us is a serious and tender place
Ourselves little flowers rather than dark spaces.

V
Gargoyles

She drinks and
He lost on the Super Bowl so
They have nothing to use to pay to
replace the engine in the car. Oh, well:
So?
Everything breaks: steps and doors.
Just to go to the first party in ages is a real hassle—
No, he says. What for? Or
she has nothing to wear. There's a tantrum next door. Oh well—
So. They go. They talk about each other to everyone—
It's their conversation. You can feel the sexy buzz,
the hum-drum of your own life drowned out, pathetic
and out of it.
Lame . . .
A chore to carry the old cardboard from the basement.
Never gets done.
The engagement ring thrown across the tile, or out the door.
It got lost the last time, so he bought her a newer and a
   bigger one
than the time before.

I guess they love each other above all marriages, don't they?
More passionate, sex more sexual, flowers
(I love you honey!) that bloom wider than yours—
Their hours spent in fights—it's more, well, real, isn't it,
than your and your spouse's subscription to the TV Guide?

The make-up over margarita and tortilla chips, fried—
gets them drunk with desire, you know? The kind
that sets them running off to Mexico, on a whim
that you could never feel, even if you tried.

You're waiting to get your washing machine repaired, when they
    re-arrive.
They convince and convince you, the friend, the relative, the
    onlooker—
The referee, oftentimes:
"I love my wife," he says, mushy-eyes, cheeks wet and alive—
It's a lot more than *you* could ever love, you boring, organized,
restrained, live-life-on-a-schedule kind of dull, neatnik, anti-
    beatnik, anal type.

The Divorce, of course, is spectacular.
How could it be otherwise?
Western Europe was utterly changed.
The phone rings. Tears flow. Custody arrangements
are *unfair*
But everyone's holidays get rearranged for the arrangement.

Who can argue with the impress
of special effects,
fireworks, and light shows?
(lots and lots and lots bigger than yours.)
Lots and lots worse than the husband's divorce, the time before.
Everyone cries, my dear.
Who could fail to sympathize, some more?

A GARGOYLE

Like a camp victim: no fat.
Tiny knees, muscles ripple down the legs, veins showing green
Like an anatomy flyleaf.
You can see her hipbones like Halloween.
Hunched over, she can barely walk, it seems.
She has no energy. Elan Vital. Libido. Nada. Zip.
What happened to her?
And frankly, she is mean.
There's the killer's gleam in her eye.
She stares with complete resignation, but no grief.
I thinks she is a freak.
I stare at her with snake fascination.
Why is she entropying?
Why is she dying like this?
I had to look into her eyes, and so I did, and gave a polite smile
But no smile back, the bitch.
I think, I guess she is too sick. I give her this.
Though I get the feeling she wouldn't give me an inch.
She talks very slow and deep, like an old woman—
I've heard her, asking, "and another thing" to the receptionist,
Whose job-smile grows then grows slim.
And her face is the death's face described by Hippocrates
Her chin a sharp cliff someone fell off of, into a murky green-
    gray ocean,
An ocean of sin.
But she is there every day, at every gym,
At every yoga studio, at every YMCA,
Gazing at the shelves inside the Vitamin place
Walking slowly walking forever down the bicycle path,
A gargoyle for the Age of the Physically Fit,
The thing we could turn ourselves into,

The starved-for perfection, the sick exorcism,
The dying-to-be-thin, middle-aged-and-still-anorexic. There
    she is,
Nearly dead, ugly as sin,
A minion from the dreaded down there.
(If you gossip just a little bit, you find out it's not Cancer.)
On the mat next to me, looking at her feet,
As we contort ourselves down deep
Into muscles, into breath and souls, I wonder where she goes,
But I remind myself to not think about her disease
But to think about my own,
To keep my eye on my own two feet,
And concentrate on the holy things
God will offer to me.

Soft, furry, cuddly people,
People who cry.
People who cry at the end of everything
("Well, it's normal!")
Every movie they tell you about they tell you they've cried.
At the end of every conversation, they cry.
Is it booze?
Is it hormonal?
Is it the huge, enormous, fake smile they give to the cameras and to
    Hellos, every other while?
Is it their furnitureless, twice-mortgaged condos, their somber ties?
Is it the vagaries of the custody battle, the divorce decree, the
    waiting in line
For the marriage license, and then for the dissolution, two times?
Fuzzy-wuzzy people,
They care a lot about things,
They listen to everything.
They listen to you spill the beans.
They offer you solace, advice.
They are very, very nice.
In fact, they are:—"nice guys."
They are:—"she has a big heart."
They are beloved in staff rooms.
They like cute cartoons.
They always give big bear-hugs.
These gentle, sweet, kinda tissuey, sweet people
Hang their shoulders low, hunch and scrunch through doorways
Have no clue about energy flow
Eat their sandwiches without a lot of show.
Most of them are not whippet-health-food-freaks
Who talk your ear off (the crazy bores!)

No. They listen. They are in recovery for behavior like that.
They are there to help.

Crying, do-gooding, freaked-out fuzzy people
Are not gentle, don't get me wrong.
They want your life, your swordlike decision making,
Your ability to move on,
And fuzzy-wuzzy tearful eyes can see things, after all.
They covet your health, and they steal your dreams,
Replicate your floor-plans, your DNA, your recipe-with-sour-
      cream.
They knock you down with an invisible body blow and say
      they're sorry for it—;

What can you do, you neutral-frown-faced person,
He sinned, and he admitted it.
The furry, cuddly guy will cry after that
("I'm so sorry!")
And everyone
Will sigh for him: he did not mean to.
He is a nation, he is a time.

MOMMY IS A SCARY NARCISSIST

C'mon, I shouldn't need to mention blepharoplasty.
Her mauled face is a part of the shared horizon.
I don't need to mention the lift, the tuck, the lipo.
(A Trinity.)
The smile-ever-smiling is a part of the position.
This is Mommy's supposition:
Sexy. Sexy. Sexy. Everlasting and in high-tonus stance. Decisions
Belong to dads, men, boyfriends, bartenders, chance.

Mommy looks good when she prays in the chapel.
(Ferns, lush foliage, candles, rose petals, and flattering paints)
Harder than the other mommies. No one stays.
(She looks into the baptismal font deeply, passionately, and long.)

Mommy tries to love, Mommy tries to get a job.
Not very hard, the outside world knows that, but Mommy
    doesn't.
In her endless, boring, yawn and anger-inducing conversations,
You, the put-upon, will know how long . . .
More than you do!
More than anyone!
She had a love affair that was *heartbreaking!*
She suffered long!
She's in this space and that design shop. She's enrolled. She's
    fragile. She talks indirectly, directly.
Shut up, Mommy!
Looking for work gives her nosebleeds, something weird and un-
    humdrum,
Disability, "bi-polar" "dis-*ease*": which could be anything,
    you see.
You rolled your eyes.

C'mon, Mommy, stop complaining! You're still young,
You said,

but Mommy knew you meant that She Looked Old.
She was able to cry soft tears then—You hurt her feelings!!
Mommy is very sad!
Now Mommy will start screaming
And Mommy is never wrong.

You shook Mommy off like a dog shaking off water!
So Mommy can cry for you all alone, which is really for the best,
For Mommy is a scary petty pest
The best, the very best of narcissists—
Look how pretty she looks praying!
Praying for you! Your soul!
All alone in the chapel—head tipped to the clouds—!
Candlelight so soft on all her faces!
Hide!
Run!

SCHMOOZE . . .

She was a flatterer.
It takes one to know one, and so was I.
So I surmised what she was up to—
The zero-in on that girl's dress "how beautiful!"
Eyes fastened on hers, chin bowed completely in submission—
I looked on, smoking a cigarette, and listened.
Who was she kidding?
She was a flatterer.
It takes one to know one, and so was I.
So: she must have surmised what I was up to?

She bathed in a milk chocolate bath with me.
She knew what to do.
You should have seen us together!
What a love-fest!
What a girl-talk without rest!
I was a very active listener.
I cocked my head like a cute munchkin.
She gave me the sexy-intense flirt eyes.
Fastened to my head while I smiled and smiled!
That's a good way for straight women to talk to each other.
And they do it this way, oh yes.
"I really like you!"
"Oh, I do too!"
Saying good-bye, like this, we said, we did.

Then there is the admission where we pretend
(A casual, noisy restaurant)
We're scared to get so close,
And that there are few people we open our hearts to—
Which is probably true, at best—.

This is probably the heart we have, the kin we belong to.
We have a cartoon heart,
We have a charming doodle for a passionate gesture,
We have libidinous, racing minds underneath the exterior.
Gifts! Gifts! Gifts! We give with all our hearts, joy, love, smarts.

So we gave each other flaccid, dewy faces
And great big hugs.
It takes one to know one, and so was I.
Therefore, we became friends forever, like lovers in love.

COLOR PHOTO

I. Father

The children were just fat thumb-suckers
Sucking up his bucks for their colleges
(He was very, very angry!)
Taking it away from his Planet Hawaii golf-self
The game of real estate and unsubtle vodka (hidden) in juice.
Drinking at the "nineteenth hole," that means,
Sucking it up. Much stuff, lots of plush, soft light, buzzed;
Money, but not money's tragedy. Not
rich *enough* for that.
Basic crass. But no tragedy. A guy-likes-to-barbecue; a 1950s
    husband
with—sheesh!—a don't-get-too-complex-on-me! bluff.
An American with a new TV
He can scream at the politicians like a true patriot.
He can motor to his patio to turn the ribs over.
He likes to channel surf.
He talks to you while he makes eye contact with the box.
Flips past the moonbeams and caterpillars fit for a kid's
    TV screen.
That's for fags, or kids.
So what?

II. Daughter

Last seen as Agnes Moorhead in *The Magnificent Ambersons.*
Invisible, but always telling you how she is.
She has friends of *all* ages.
Takes a cheerful two-week vacation toward Bali, Tahiti, Majorca.

Who will care for her in her old age?
Insurance is not her thing.
Three husbands, each weaker than the previous and registering
    astonishment on their faces after they figured things out,
could not keep her.
She lives off the resentful charity of her betters.
She accepts pity, and knows that people feel responsible.
They enlist in her cause.
They try to fix her up, like distressed real estate.
For what?
Oh, don't get me wrong: she has a degree, and a job, and a clean,
    up-to-date hair style and wardrobe.
She gets her nails done.
Spinster aunts, maiden aunts, they don't exist anymore, you
    think.
Independent women, some are called today.
Yeah, she's seen a shrink.
She is
hiding bottles under the sink, there have become so many. It's
"Not what you think."
But everyone feels *sorry*.

He was not a kind man.
Tender would be a word he would wince at.
I think he could have had sex with any woman he desired.
He was like a man from a bodice ripper—
"Handsome, devastating."
As far as I can tell you,
He was into the seduction,
Was what they used to call a rake,
Left the women "seduced and abandoned."
You know people like this.
If you don't, you're lucky.
No one turned his head.
He sneered at women for wanting him: their foolishness was so
    embarrassing.
He could have sex by leaning the girl over a trashcan.
I didn't even think that was too weird, when I heard of it.
I knew people like this.
I knew people who routinely referred to each other as dirty words.
You know people like this.
If you don't, you're lucky.
He met a woman.
He spent the night with her.
He was ready to leave in the morning when she started to tell him
    about a book she'd read.
He'd read it; he'd never met another person who had.
They held each other, in that way of good feeling.
At that moment, his heart opened just a little bit
(—The space between the hands of the Virgin Mary, when they're
    held in front of her chest—)
Small, but big enough for a small light to shine out of.
His heart opened, and this woman happened to be there.

It could have been another woman, another place.
His time had come.
Sorry, the marriage between them didn't last.
When she left him, he felt sad, with a sadness that befits a small
    opening
With a large and benevolent protectiveness around it.
He was protected.
He couldn't endure much.
After a long time, I think he will get another chance.
Maybe another kind of love for his heart.
I'm writing his story, and I've heard
That some people, when their hearts open,
They rain stones onto the floor,
Gold coins fly like those from the jackpot of a slot machine,
A frightening and unendurable joy: I know
Some people feel their ribs widen and their bodies rack
with sobs, for how long it's taken.

COMMENCEMENT ADDRESS

I have no more to say about throwing up or causing myself to get diarrhea there's nothing heroic about it though the movies on TV want us to endure quietly and cry appropriately. It's a wonderful role for any young actress to place herself in some dead household where the dialogue is sexual between all of them including dead grandparents who are still alive in theory and very much inside everyone's bodies, clucking away like old geezers with huge inflated egos bruised by the failure of their children to spend each moment worshipping their self-created sun. So the girl you see who opens her legs to the idea of fucking everyone who says hello but also wants to feel like a nun with vaginal orgasms rather than the ones his kisses and teeth cause which seemed to come to e.g., Saint Thérèse the Little Flower just from prayer in her cloister for hours which made the girl, the subject of this poem, cry for its truth and its nakedness. Because how could it be good to have that curly-haired boy put his face between your legs nearly every afternoon who will not even say he loves you and this is what your parents don't like about it: he will not spend his money on you or take you places in his car. But of course we have to learn to live inside fences and to sweep and clean lower our heads until in the end it is this which gives me flutters I do not need his teeth and lips at my sacred entrance I find release in order and demure discipline the needle and thread tongue-tied when you accept that you do not have this choice if you become a slut, after you see the error of your ways, you renounce them, you become someone who will live easily within his four walls where he keeps you like the flame of love inside his body there's no need to find the way out this is the way it will be and always was: all the mirrors around you say sacrifice order and love.

"They rain stones onto the floor" in the poem Agapé: I got this idea and the inspiration for this poem from Shirley Jackson's novel *The Haunting of Hill House*: ". . . one day, when she was twelve years old and her sister was eighteen, and their father had been dead for not quite a month, showers of stones had fallen on their house, without any warning or any indication of purpose or reason, dropping from the ceilings, rolling loudly down the walls, breaking windows and pattering maddeningly on the roof. . . ." (*The Haunting of Hill House*, New York: Warner Books, 1982, pp. 7–8.)

The poem "Poetry" is dedicated to George Starbuck, 1931–1996.

Juan Delgado, *Green Web*
Wayne Dodd, *Echoes of the Unspoken*
Wayne Dodd, *Sometimes Music Rises*
Joseph Duemer, *Customs*
Candice Favilla, *Cups*
Casey Finch, *Harming Others*
Norman Finkelstein, *Restless Messengers*
Dennis Finnell, *Belovèd Beast*
Karen Fish, *The Cedar Canoe*
Albert Goldbarth, *Heaven and Earth: A Cosmology*
Pamela Gross, *Birds of the Night Sky/Stars of the Field*
Kathleen Halme, *Every Substance Clothed*
Jonathan Holden, *American Gothic*
Paul Hoover, *Viridian*
Austin Hummell, *The Fugitive Kind*
Claudia Keelan, *The Secularist*
Maurice Kilwein Guevara, *Postmortem*
Caroline Knox, *To Newfoundland*
Steve Kronen, *Empirical Evidence*
Patrick Lawler, *A Drowning Man Is Never Tall Enough*
Sydney Lea, *No Sign*
Jeanne Lebow, *The Outlaw James Copeland and the Champion-Belted Empress*
Phillis Levin, *Temples and Fields*
Gary Margolis, *Falling Awake*
Mark McMorris, *The Black Reeds*
Jacqueline Osherow, *Conversations with Survivors*
Jacqueline Osherow, *Looking for Angels in New York*
Tracy Philpot, *Incorrect Distances*
Donald Revell, *The Gaza of Winter*
Martha Ronk, *Desire in L.A.*
Martha Ronk, *Eyetrouble*
Aleda Shirley, *Chinese Architecture*
Pamela Stewart, *The Red Window*
Susan Stewart, *The Hive*
Terese Svoboda, *All Aberration*
Terese Svoboda, *Mere Mortals*
Lee Upton, *Approximate Darling*
Arthur Vogelsang, *Twentieth Century Women*
Sidney Wade, *Empty Sleeves*
Marjorie Welish, *Casting Sequences*
Susan Wheeler, *Bag 'o' Diamonds*
C. D. Wright, *String Light*
Katayoon Zandvakili, *Deer Table Legs*